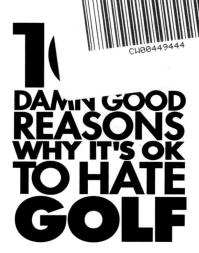

10 DAMN GOOD REASONS WHY IT'S OK TO HATE GOLF

CW00449444

1

Golfers chase the ball for miles. Not even dogs are that stupid...

2

Golf is just an excuse for men to fiddle with another set of balls...

3

Golf is deadly - many players have been struck by lightning. Unfortunately – not nearly enough of them...

During a game, the only reason that people clap is in a desperate attempt to stay awake...

5

With golf, you don't play to win. You play to make business deals...

6

The only way to get your ball over a water hazard is to play a course that has no water hazards...

The only aerobic exercise you really get from golf is by jumping up and down on your club...

Because if there's one tree on a 4-acre course, your ball is guaranteed to hit it...

9

Because you'd get more exercise walking around a phone box...

10

Not content with wearing ridiculous hats themselves, some players force their poor golf clubs to wear them too...

11

Golfing sweaters must be designed by
color-blind grannies...

13

You spend so much time searching the woods your nickname is Little Red Riding Hood...

Golf fanatics have a million reasons for that lousy shot; the water hazard, the bunker, the gravitational pull of the moon...

15

Golf commentators who talk in awed, hushed voices as though they're witnessing a miracle...

Chequered slacks, just short enough to reveal those furry lemon socks...

17

The only point of a practice swing is
that it's a chance for you to practice
looking like an idiot when you miss the
real swing...

18

The golfer who wields his club as though he's Russell Crowe in *Gladiator*...

19

Because a man will never remember his
wedding anniversary, but he'll sure as hell
remember his score, five holes back should
be four, not five...

20

Jack Nicklaus's nickname was 'The Golden Bear'. Greg Norman's was 'The Great White Shark'. You have one too. It's 'Jabba the Putt'...

21

Mark Twain said; 'Golf is a good walk spoiled'. Except golfers don't even walk anymore, they use carts…

22

The real reason why Executive Courses are short is that your job depends on letting the boss win, so why prolong the charade?

23

The longer you take to carefully line up a putt, the more certain you are to miss it...

After a lousy game you fantasize about being a caddie. You'd get fit from lugging the clubs about, but you'd also get to snigger at players like you...

25

Golf courses have such snooty names. The Royal and Ancient Golf Club of St Andrew was actually originally a sheep pasture...

26

A golfer will boast about his only hole in one, and fail to mention it was a hole in one day…

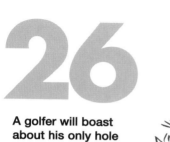

27

You spend more time scrabbling round for
lost balls than actually playing...

A classic shot is always followed by the worst shot in history...

29

Golf turns you into the sort of person you used to laugh at in school; a nerd who cheats...

When your golfing partner says 'Tough break' you can be sure he really means 'Stevie Wonder could have got that shot, you loser'...

31

The 'expert' who's free with advice which
somehow never improves your game...

32

Your sworn enemy always plays better than you do. (By the way, when you started the game you were best friends...)

33

Golf is like nicotine; addictive, expensive and you're always swearing to give it up...

34

You've spent more time in the sand than Moses...

35

You've lost more balls than the veterinarian's neutering department...

36

You can be hopeless at golf and sex. But at least you can enjoy being bad at sex!

37

If your opponent keeps quoting the rules, he's definitely cheating (especially if he's winning)...

38

Golf is masochism without the attractive leatherwear…

39

There is always one player that talks to you during your backswing…

You can spot a golf fanatic a mile off...

41

Determined to be a good sportsman, you insist on playing the ball where it lies...

Your golf partner is asked what his handicap is, and he points to you...

Experts say you should only keep one swing thought in your mind at a time. Trouble is it's always the same thought: 'Oh please don't let me miss, please don't let me miss'...

Scary knickerbockers tucked into diamond-patterned knee socks. Not only are they ridiculous but it's also harder to hide a few extra golf balls up your trousers...

Fifteenth-century Scotsmen originally played golf wearing tights and puffed breeches. The only difference now is that the clothes aren't nearly so stylish...

Businessmen take up golf to relieve
corporate stress and end up longing for a
nice relaxing hostile takeover...

47

Your opponent remarks that you play golf
like Kevin Costner, and just as you're starting
to preen, adds…"in *Waterworld*"…

If your IQ were as high as your golf score, you'd be telling Stephen Hawking where he was going wrong...

Hazards are to golf balls what Elizabeth Taylor is to husbands...

50

The biggest hazard on the golf course is you...

51

The only possible way of improving your game is to have started earlier than Tiger Woods. (He picked up his first club at nine months by the way…)

Golfers' elbow...

53

Golfing psychologists say it's vital to develop a 'strong memory pattern' for an effortless back swing. But what do you do when your memory pattern is stuck '★★★★, Il've missed again'?

Golf twists your values. You allow your rotten boss to win, but won't concede a single putt to your best friend...

55

You've spent so much time flinging your clubs about that someone suggests you take up the javelin...

56

Dave Hill likened the accurate golf swing
to sex. Could that be why so many golfers
fumble about, then miss?

You think that the terms 'semi-rough' and 'rough' are shorthand for the two types of game you play...

58

In desperation, you ask a therapist how to improve your game and he says: 'Stop playing it'...

59

Golf is like going to an S&M club. You can always find someone to beat you...

A golf expert suggests you don't fight the wind but use it to shape and direct the shot. And how did this help Tommy Bolt? When he broke wind, all he got was a fine!

Golf is an outdoor retirement home for
politicians and variety club acts...

62

A friendly match nearly always ends up as a screaming match...

Golf is a game of two halves. In the first half, you think 'At least I'm not playing as badly as last time', and in the second half you think 'No I'm playing worse'...

Golf is a game where you quickly lose your balls, and slowly lose your marbles...

65

Because Billy Graham wore yellow pigskin golf shoes on the course. God may forgive him, but we, the fashion police, cannot...

When a wild rocker like Alice Cooper plays golf, you know he's one step away from false teeth and a wig...

All your memorable rounds take place in the
club bar…

Because balls that plop into short holes develop a sudden ability to bounce straight out again...

Your brains are so scrambled that when an opponent asks you what ball you're playing, you reply 'Er the small round one?'

An opponent describes you as a 'latter day Alan Shepard', the first man to play golf on the moon. 'Because you play golf like you're on another planet'...

71

Reverend Billy Graham's complaint that God never answered his prayers on the course, is proof that even God hates golf...

72

The only reason so many politicians play is because it's the perfect training ground for lying, cheating, and getting out of a hole...

73

The only use for a golfing umbrella is to hold weddings under it...

Every three-par hole has the power to expand, contract and shift. Like something out of the *X Files*…

75

You know where Lyndon Johnson was coming from when he remarked: 'I don't have a handicap. I'm all handicap'...

76

Nobody ever wants to hear about your golfing triumphs. They'll listen agog at your disasters and ineptitude for hours though...

In *The Legend of Bagger Vance*, the golf stroke is a metaphor for life. So, hard as you try to keep your eye on the ball, you'll still end up in a hole covered in earth and wearing bad trousers...

You are promoted to the board and then
have to spend your entire pay rise on an
expensive set of golf clubs...

79

The mechanized golf club, patented in 1942 'applauded' a good swing, and blew a raspberry at a bad one. What other sport could invent such a finely honed torment, one where the player is mocked by his own equipment?

Because you rarely get streakers in baseball or soccer. It says something about the dullness of golf, that often, the only thing of interest on the green is some saggy-bottomed exhibitionist, running around aimlessly…

Being bitten by the golf bug is like a malaria bite. You become hot, sweaty and feverish and start babbling nonsense. In extreme cases the only way out is death...

All a golfer has to do to get a fine is to wear long trousers on a hot day...

The mad golfing terminology. Divot, birdy, bogey and shagbag. They sound more like the names of cartoon dogs...

84

Why do golfers need so many clubs?
You don't see a pitcher nipping off for
a lighter ball...

Laddie Lucas and Jim England would sometimes demonstrate their swing by wearing blindfolds. Pair of show-offs. You always play like you're blindfolded...

86

If God had meant us to play golf, He would have bulldozed the Garden of Eden, cut down the trees and turned it into a celestial putting green...

87

Because clubs revenge
themselves. Bobby
Cruickshank once
victoriously, threw his
club into the air. It
promptly fell on his
head, knocking him
out cold...

The golf shop recognizes you as the one who's always returning clubs because they 'somehow keep snapping in half'...

89

Because no matter how rich you are, you can't buy a golf swing...

Not even Jesus could deal with water hazards. He might have walked on water, but nowhere in the New Testament does it say he got his golf ball back...

Because golf professionals are so rich!
They don't even have the decency to blow
it on fast cars and loose living, which might
make the rest of us feel a bit better...

Because British golfer Mark James believed
his putter was possessed by an evil spirit.
Hey, you know your putter has an evil streak.
It's the only explanation for the ball spinning
360 degrees and the unholy mess you keep
making of the turf...

93

Golf kicks everything off the television schedules. You set your video for what you think is a triple episode of ER and return home to find you've recorded five interminable hours of badly dressed men hitting something with a stick...

The snobbery…

95

'Hilarious' car stickers that read: 'If you think I'm a bad driver, you should see my golf'. At least a bad driver gets his license revoked....

The 500 forms that you need to fill in to get a membership card…

Skateboards go faster than golfcarts...

The only golf tip you can ever remember is from Stewart Maiden. 'Hit 'em hard. They'll land somewhere'...

99

When you've played a ridiculous shot there is no where to run except to the next...

The local course offers not only a list of
tee-off times but also sound-off and
storm-off times too....

LAGOON
BOOKS

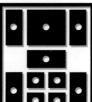